My
Toddler Knows
All About
Butterfly
Bb For Butterfly
Alwina Kindo

Bb
For
Butterfly
My Toddler
knows about
Butterfly
Alwina2 Kindo

This
Book
Belongs To
Name

Dedicated to

My Husband and Four precious gems Aakash, Adithya, Abishek and
Sparsha. You make me so proud. Always be the best you can be.
-Mommy

Picture Credits
Pixabay.com, Google images Creative Commons

Book Info
This book introduces the life cycle of a butterfly to the toddler, its life cylce ,
it different size, color and its importance. The images, repetition of words
and phrases support early readers and help the early readers to
understand the text. This book introduces early readers to subject - specific
vocabulary words. Toddlers or some early readers may need some
assistance to read some of the words.

B for Butterfly

Butterfly is very beautiful

I belong to the insect family

I love flowers

I use my long tongue to sip the nectar from flowers

I always never looked like this

My life began as a tiny egg

Then I hatched in few days

I came out as a caterpillar

I was very hungry so I ate up
the egg shell

Was still hungry so I ate leaves

And ate more leaves

I ate and grew...

And ate, and ate and grew

I was ready to change so I
hung from a branch

And turned into a pupa

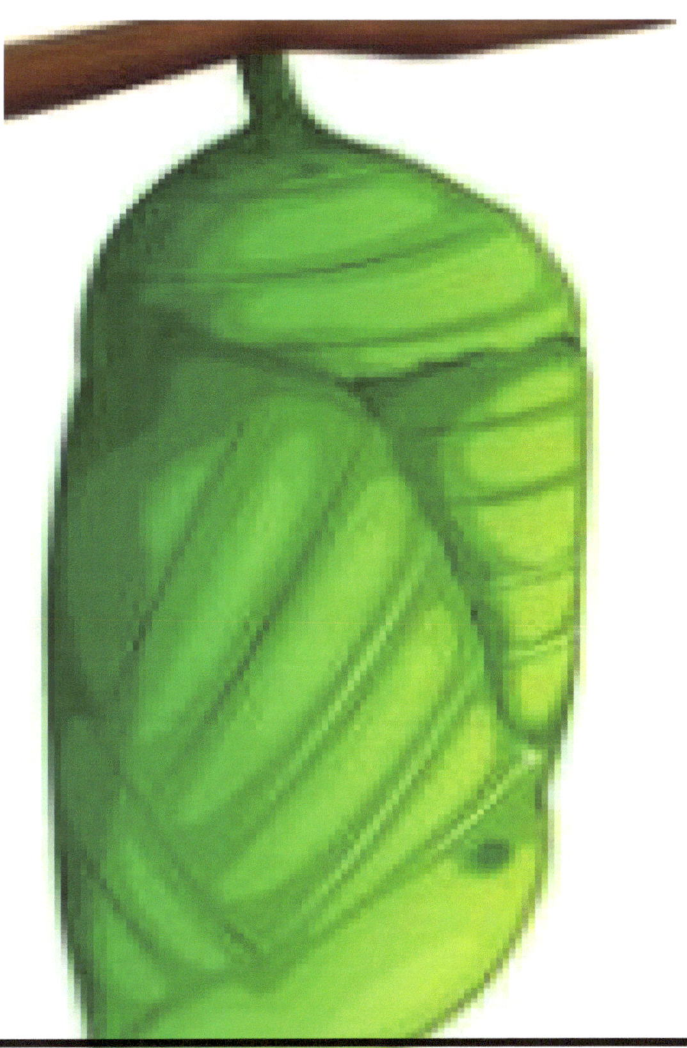

Which is in a form of a hard shell

On the outside the pupa
looked very still

But on the inside there was a lot going on

And then one fine day I came out.

My wings were wet and crumpled.

After few hours my wings were dry.

Now I have strong wings.

I can fly.

Guess where I am going?

Hope you enjoyed the book.